VELOCITY™

AMERICAN SPECIAL OPS

THE U.S. NAVY SEALS
The Missions

by Jennifer M. Besel

Consultant:
Michael A. Raney
Force Public Affairs Leading Chief
Petty Officer, Commander
Naval Special Warfare Command
San Diego, California

CAPSTONE PRESS
a capstone imprint

Velocity is published by Capstone Press,
1710 Roe Crest Drive, North Mankato, Minnesota 56003.
www.capstonepub.com

Library of Congress Cataloging-in-Publication Data
Besel, Jennifer M.
The U.S. Navy SEALs : the missions / by Jennifer M. Besel.
pages cm. —(Velocity. American Special Ops)
Includes bibliographical references and index.
Summary: "Describes the U.S. Navy SEALs, including their history, weapons, gear,
     and missions"—Provided by publisher.
ISBN 978-1-4296-8715-7 (library binding)
ISBN 978-1-62065-357-9 (ebook PDF)
1. United States. Navy. SEALs—Juvenile literature. 2. United States. Navy—
Commando troops—Juvenile literature. I. Title. II. Title: United States Navy SEALs.
VG87.B393 2013
359.9'84—dc23   2011053142

Editorial Credits
Carrie Braulick Sheely, editor; Veronica Correia, designer; Laura Manthe,
     production specialist

Photo Credits
AP Images: Luke Frazza, Pool, 13; Shutterstock: Atlaspix, 30, ildogesto, 6-7 (world
map), iQoncept, 14-15, JustASC, 10, Makhnach, 6-7 (radar grid), Olinchuk, 16,
RCPPHOTO, 28, Ridvan EFE, 11; U.S. Marine Corps photo by Lcpl. Kevin C. Quihuis,
32, Lcpl. Megan E. Sindelar, 31; U.S. Navy Photo, 20, 39 (bottom), 40, 42 (top),
44-45, by JO1 Steve Orr, 12, MC2 Arcenio Gonzalez Jr., 36-37, MC2 Dominique M.
Lasco, 23 (right inset), MC2 Eddie Harrison, 8, MC2 Erika N. Jones, 27 (bottom),
MC2 Erika N. Manzano, 27 (top), MC2 Joshua T. Rodriquez, 4-5, MC2 Kyle D.
Gahlau, 1, 22, 23 (left inset), MC2 Marcos T. Hernandez, 21 (bottom right), MC2
Matt Daniels, 17, MC2 Michelle Kapica, 21 (middle inset), MC2 Shauntae Hinkle,
21 (top inset), MC2 Zane Ecklund, 33 (bottom), MC3 Blake Midnight, 23, MC3
Michelle L. Kapica, 34, PH1 Keith W. DeVinney, 24, PH1 Tim Turner, 9, PH2 Eric
Powell, 29 (bottom), PH2 Eric S. Logsdon, 21 (bottom), 37 (bottom), PH2 USNR-R
Milton Savage, 29 (top), PHAN John P. Curtis, 33 (top), PHCS Andrew McKaskle,
35, 38, 39 (top), 41, 26, cover; United States Department of Defense, 42 (bottom);
Wikipedia/Michael Dorosh, 29 (middle)

Artistic Effects
Shutterstock

Printed in the United States of America in Stevens Point, Wisconsin.

TABLE OF CONTENTS

T 17919

WORLDWIDE WARRIORS

Hundreds of miles from land, a group of highly-trained military men drops into the Pacific Ocean. Halfway around the world, another group of fighters slithers through weeds in a murky swamp. To accomplish their missions, these men fast-rope from helicopters, speed across water in boats, and sneak into enemy territory. They aren't just ordinary fighters. They are U.S. Navy SEALs.

On any day, Navy SEALs are **deployed** in more than 30 countries around the world. They are sent on dangerous missions where a large force cannot fight. Small teams of SEALs can enter enemy territory from the sea, air, or land. In fact, SEAL stands for sea, air, and land.

The Navy SEALs are an elite special operations group. SEALs need to be brave, smart, quick, and highly trained. Very few men who start SEAL training complete it to become SEALs. The United States relies on the ones who do to carry out some of the country's most important and dangerous missions.

fast-rope—to quickly descend from a helicopter to the ground using a rope

deploy—to be put in place for a mission or battle

Chapter 1

ON THE JOB

SEAL teams travel around the world, often in secret. The leaders who sent them are usually the only ones who know where the SEALs are and what their mission is.

THROUGHOUT THEIR HISTORY, SEALs HAVE PLAYED MANY IMPORTANT ROLES IN WARS AND CONFLICTS AROUND THE WORLD.

VIETNAM WAR

VIETNAM — 1959–1975

SEALs were some of the first American fighters in Vietnam at the start of the Vietnam War. SEAL teams trained South Vietnamese soldiers to do secret missions. SEALs also went on many direct combat missions.

OPERATION JUST CAUSE

PANAMA — 1989

By the fall of 1989, Panama's leader Manuel Noriega was struggling to stay in power. His troops attacked U.S. forces and citizens in the country. Several Americans were killed, wounded, or captured. SEALs and other special ops teams invaded Panama. A team of 48 SEALs landed on the beach near an airfield. The SEALs battled with enemy soldiers and eventually took control of the airfield. They also destroyed enemy patrol boats, which kept Noriega from using them to escape.

Getting Orders

The approximately 2,400 active SEALs get mission assignments through a detailed process. SEALs are part of a larger group called Naval Special Warfare (NSW). NSW is responsible for training SEALs. The NSW also coordinates boat teams and other support for SEALs.

NSW is part of the United States Special Operations Command (USSOCOM). This group organizes all U.S. special ops teams from the Navy, Army, Marines, and Air Force. Members of USSOCOM decide which teams are best for each mission.

Mission goals are sent to USSOCOM from the U.S. Department of Defense (DOD). And where does the DOD get its orders? Those orders come directly from the U.S. president.

OPERATION ENDURING FREEDOM

AFGHANISTAN — OCTOBER 2001-PRESENT

On September 11, 2001, al-Qaida terrorists hijacked American passenger planes. Two jets were flown into the World Trade Center in New York City. Another plane was flown into the Pentagon in Washington, D.C. A fourth plane crashed in a Pennsylvania field. Some people think it may have been headed for the White House. After the attacks, SEALs were put on the ground in Afghanistan, where the al-Qaida group was based. The SEALs found terrorists' weapons supplies hidden in caves. SEALs destroyed more than 500,000 pounds (226,800 kilograms) of weapons. SEAL teams also stopped many terrorists who were trying to leave the country by sea.

OPERATION IRAQI FREEDOM

IRAQ — MARCH 20, 2003-AUGUST 2010

SEALs played a large role in the war in Iraq. SEAL teams protected oil and off-shore gas terminals. They raided warehouses, searching for dangerous weapons. SEALs also conducted a prisoner of war rescue.

terrorist—a person who uses threats, force, or attacks to frighten or harm others

ON A MISSION

SEALs complete extensive training. This training creates skilled fighters who can do a variety of missions. SEAL missions range from direct action to reconnaissance.

Direct Action

SEALs on direct action missions are ready to attack. SEALs strike enemy targets with weapons and are directly in the line of fire. Teams may use ambushes and raids to stop enemies. For an ambush, soldiers hide and wait until the enemy comes to them. Then they attack the enemy by surprise. In a raid, SEALs also use the element of surprise by attacking quickly with a small force of men.

Fact

Some SEAL sniper guns reach targets more than 0.5 mile (0.8 kilometer) away.

reconnaissance—a mission to gather information about an enemy

Special Reconnaissance

Reconnaissance missions are designed to gather information. SEALs sneak behind enemy lines to learn:

- how many soldiers the enemy has.
- how many weapons the enemy has and where they are stored.
- where the enemy is located and if there are plans to move.
- about the landscape, including the condition of beaches and water in the area.

Teams send the information they gather back to NSW and USSOCOM. Leaders then plan missions using the information.

Navy SEALs do special reconnaissance on a suspected terrorist location in Afghanistan in 2002.

9

SEAL OBJECTIVE: Conduct a diversion operation off the coast of Kuwait during Operation Desert Storm.

DATE OF MISSION: February 23, 1991

BACKGROUND: In August 1990 Iraqi forces invaded Kuwait. The United Nations, including the United States, demanded that Iraq leave Kuwait by January 15, 1991. Iraq refused.

On January 17 U.S.-led forces began air strikes against Iraqi targets. After a month of air strikes, troops were put in place for a ground assault.

diversion—something that distracts from something else
assault—a violent attack

Step 1: During the air strikes, U.S. ships went to the Persian Gulf east of Kuwait. At least 17,000 Marines and one SEAL team were on these ships.

Step 2: Under the cover of darkness on February 23, six SEALs took landing boats from the ships to within 500 yards (457 m) of a Kuwaiti beach.

Iraq

Persian Gulf

Kuwait

Step 3: The SEALs left their landing boats and swam to shore. Each man towed a 20-pound (9-kg) case of explosives.

Step 4: On shore, the SEALs rigged the explosives on the beach. They set them to explode at 1:00 a.m. Then the SEALs went back to the boats.

Step 5: At 1:00 a.m. the explosives went off as expected. The SEALs fired grenades at the shore. The noise and ships in the Gulf convinced Iraqi soldiers that the U.S. Navy was attacking them. The Iraqis moved two army divisions to cover the shore.

Step 6: When the Iraqis reached the shore, they found that all the ships and the SEALs had left. Far inland, Marines and other forces attacked the Iraqi troops that had stayed. The ground war then began against a divided Iraqi force.

Counterterrorism

Terrorism is a huge threat to countries around the world. On counterterrorism missions, SEALs capture terrorists and try to keep their plans from succeeding.

In March 2002 several special ops teams were sent to Afghanistan. Their goal was to capture al-Qaida terrorists in the Shah-i-Kot Valley. SEALs snuck into the mountains. One team found an enemy machine gun post that U.S. aircraft had missed. The SEALs quickly called in an air strike that destroyed the enemy's position.

Women and Special Forces

Federal law does not allow women to be in units that serve in direct ground combat roles. Women can't become Navy SEALs. However, some women support the SEALs and other U.S. special forces. More than 400 women serve with the Navy's special operations forces. Their positions include intelligence analysts, legal specialists, and builders. In Afghanistan women have been serving alongside special forces units in cultural support roles. They help local women understand the mission of U.S. forces in the country.

Foreign Internal Defense

Many countries are under the threat of terrorism or struggle against drug warlords. But they have no way to defend themselves. SEALs can help in these situations. On foreign internal defense missions, SEALs teach other countries' armies. SEALs teach foreign soldiers war tactics that can be used on rivers and coastlines. SEALs also provide weapons and medical training to foreign troops. With the training SEALs provide, nations are better able to defend themselves against threats. SEALs have conducted foreign internal defense missions with partner nations throughout the world.

Navy SEALs provide machine gun training to Peruvian soldiers.

Unconventional Warfare

Using local people to fight an enemy can be very effective. Enemies rarely suspect that people from their own country are tricking them. This type of mission is known as unconventional warfare. SEALs might train the local people to collect **intelligence** and conduct **sabotage** missions.

intelligence—secret information about an enemy's plans or actions
sabotage—damage or destruction of property that is done on purpose

Chapter 2

REVVING UP

The SEALs grew out of powerful groups that helped the United States and its allies win World War II. These groups no longer exist. But some of the skills and lessons the groups learned are still taught to SEALs.

Fact

Underwater Demolition Teams earned a couple of nicknames during World War II. Some people called them "naked warriors." But the name that stuck was "frogmen." SEALs are often called frogmen today.

Amphibious Scouts and Raiders

The Amphibious Scouts and Raiders formed during World War II as a beach reconnaissance force. These soldiers surveyed beaches. They used the information they gathered to help large forces use the beaches for attacks.

AUGUST 1942

Naval Combat Demolition Units [NCDUs]

NCDUs were trained to carry out demolitions, use explosives, and conduct raids near water. However, these men had to do all their work in shallow water. They were ordered to wear full gear and stay out of the water as much as possible. The men paddled into enemy territory in rubber boats. They disarmed enemy explosives and set their own explosives.

JUNE 1943

Operational Swimmers of the Office of Strategic Services [OSS]

Some OSS soldiers became experts at combat swimming. They used their skills to dive underwater. They often attached mines with magnets to enemy ships. The mines were set to explode after a certain amount of time.

NOVEMBER 1943

Underwater Demolition Teams [UDTs]

UDTs were formed to do reconnaissance like the Scouts and Raiders and do underwater explosive work like the NCDUs. But the training for UDTs focused heavily on developing strong swimmers. No longer did the men have to wear full gear and stay out of the water. Instead, these men wore swimsuits, face masks, and fins. They planted underwater explosives to protect landing beaches.

NOVEMBER 1943

demolition—the blowing up of or the taking down of a structure on purpose

UDTs in KOREA

The U.S. government broke up all the water combat teams after World War II. But just five years later, UDTs were once again called into action.

In 1950 North Korea invaded South Korea. The United States sent soldiers to help South Korea, including 300 UDTs. The UDTs did beach reconnaissance, destroyed enemy bridges, and raided enemy railroad tunnels along the coast. UDT operations during the Korean War (1950–1953) included:

Operation Fishnet

U.S. military leaders wanted to reduce North Korea's food supply to make it harder to feed the country's soldiers. UDTs worked along the North Korean coast, diving underwater to destroy fishing nets. They also helped sink several small fishing boats.

Operation Chromite

This operation was aimed at taking back the South Korean capital city of Seoul. The U.S. military planned to enter Seoul through the port city of Incheon, which was about 20 miles (32 km) from Seoul. UDTs went in ahead of the Marines to look for mines and low areas of water where ships could get stuck. UDTs also acted as guides for the Marine attack.

Wonsan Harbor

On October 12, 1950, two U.S. ships hit mines and sank. UDTs rescued 25 sailors from the sinking vessels.

NORTH KOREA

SOUTH KOREA

Ch'ongjin

Hyesan

Kanggye

Sinuiju

Sain-ni

P'yongyang

Namp'o

Sariwon

Haeju

Kaesong

Ch'unch'on

Seoul

Ch'ongju

Taejon

Chonju

Taegu

Kwangju

Pusan

Koje-do

Chin-do

16

FROM UDT  TO SEAL

Beginning in the late 1950s, Navy leaders saw a need for fighters trained in unconventional warfare. By May 1961, a plan for a new force called the SEALs was in place. In January 1962 President John F. Kennedy announced to the public that the country would meet this growing need for special ops fighters. The SEALs were formed to handle special operations on the water. UDT members were selected as the first SEALs, forming the first two SEAL teams.

Almost immediately, SEALs were sent to fight in the Mekong Delta in the Vietnam War (1959–1975). They conducted highly dangerous direct-action missions against the enemy group known as the Viet Cong.

Fact

During the Vietnam War, the Viet Cong called SEALs "the men with the green faces."

SEALs perform a demonstration at an event to honor the SEALs' history in 2010.

Chapter 3

BECOMING A SEAL

Becoming a SEAL takes not only strength and intelligence, but an unchanging commitment. The training sailors go through pushes them to their physical and mental limits.

If you want to be a Navy SEAL, here's what you can expect.

START HERE

JOIN THE NAVY

The first step to becoming a SEAL is joining the Navy. To join, you must meet these requirements:
- be between 17 and 34 years old; to be a SEAL you must be under 28 years old. But age waivers can be obtained for those up to 30 years old.
- be a U.S. citizen
- have your high school diploma or GED
- be drug and alcohol free

NOT QUALIFIED   QUALIFIED

You are not accepted into the Navy. The path to becoming a SEAL ends here.

Your SEAL contract is denied. You will be sent to Recruit Training Command (RTC) to be trained for other Navy jobs.

ASK FOR A SEAL CONTRACT

When joining the Navy, tell your recruiter that you want to become a SEAL. The recruiter will give you a Physical Screening Test (PST). To continue on the path to becoming a SEAL, you must meet these requirements:
- swim 500 yards (457 meters) in less than 12 minutes, 30 seconds
- do 42 push-ups in two minutes
- do 50 sit-ups in two minutes
- run 1.5 miles (2.4 km) in less than 11 minutes
- do 6 pull-ups

NOT QUALIFIED   QUALIFIED

CONGRATULATIONS! YOU ARE A NAVY SEAL!

QUALIFIED

GO TO SEAL QUALIFICATION TRAINING (SQT)

In SQT you'll learn what it takes to do the job of a SEAL. In this 26-week training program, you'll learn everything from cold-weather survival to combat mission skills.

For more details on SQT, turn to page 26.

NOT QUALIFIED

QUALIFIED

GO TO JUMP SCHOOL

If you pass BUD/S, you'll move on to three weeks of basic parachute training. To pass this training, you must complete a series of jumps. The final jump must be done at night with full combat gear from at least 9,500 feet (2,896 m) high.

For more details on Jump School, turn to page 24.

NOT QUALIFIED

You are reassigned to another Navy job. The path to becoming a SEAL ends here, but you may reapply after serving in other Navy positions.

QUALIFIED

ASSIGNMENT TO BASIC UNDERWATER DEMOLITION/SEAL (BUD/S)

BUD/S is one of the hardest training programs in the world. More than two-thirds of any class quits before the end of the six-month course.

For more details on BUD/S, turn to page 20.

NOT QUALIFIED

GO TO "A" SCHOOL

After RTC, you'll go to a prep school to get in-depth technical training. Depending on your career track, you'll go to one of several schools. Here are just a few of them:
• Center for Surface Combat Systems
• Center for Anti-Terrorism and Navy Security Forces
• Center for Submarine Learning
• Center for Explosive Ordinance Disposal (EOD)/Diving

GO TO RECRUIT TRAINING COMMAND (RTC)

Also known as boot camp, this phase gets all new recruits ready for life in the Navy. Recruits with a SEAL contract must pass the PST again by the sixth week of RTC.

NOT QUALIFIED

QUALIFIED

You are released from your SEAL contract. You will be trained for other Navy jobs. But the path to becoming a SEAL ends here.

19

BUD/S

Becoming a Navy SEAL takes an enormous amount of dedication. By the end of "A" school, sailors working toward this goal have been through hours of testing and training. But they have never experienced anything like BUD/S training.

BUD/S training will bring sailors to their breaking points. It isn't just physically tough. It's also mentally and emotionally draining. Most men who enter BUD/S later decide to quit, which is called dropping on request (DOR). Those who complete it are one step closer to becoming a SEAL.

Before a sailor even gets to the BUD/S training exercises, he must go through Naval Special Warfare Preparatory School. The prep school lasts for two months. The goal is to prepare sailors for the intense training they will go through in BUD/S. At the end of prep school, the men must pass another PST. But this one is much harder. Each sailor must:

do a 3,280-foot (1,000-m) swim with fins in under 20 minutes.

do at least 70 push-ups in two minutes.

do at least 10 pull-ups.

do at least 60 sit-ups in two minutes.

do a 4-mile (6-km) run in less than 31 minutes.

If a sailor doesn't pass this PST, he is dropped from the training and assigned a different Navy job.

Fact

Only about 26 percent of sailors complete BUD/S training. Many DOR, and others cannot complete the training because of injuries.

TRAINING FOCUS: physical conditioning
TRAINING LENGTH: seven weeks
TRAINING LOCATION: Coronado, California

Weeks 1–3

The first three weeks sailors focus on physical conditioning, teamwork, and becoming experts in the water. The men run, do push-ups, swim, and wind through obstacle courses. Teams race carrying 300-pound (136-kg) logs. They learn to use small boats. The men also must pass "drown-proofing." In this training, they learn to swim with their hands and feet tied up.

Week 4

The first weeks prepare the men for the fourth week of training. This week is the men's ultimate test of physical and mental strength. In five and a half days, they get no more than four hours of sleep. During the same period of time, they train 20 hours a day and run more than 200 miles (322 km). Men can DOR at any time, and many do so this week.

Weeks 5–7

Those who complete week four go on to learn how to conduct underwater survey operations. This training teaches the men how to chart the sea floor. The sailors also learn to look for human-made or natural structures that could get in the way of an attack.

During week four, sailors who want to drop on request do so by ringing a bell that is always nearby.

Second Phase

TRAINING FOCUS: combat diving
TRAINING LENGTH: seven weeks
TRAINING LOCATION: Coronado, California

During the second phase of BUD/S, the men learn diving skills they will use in combat. This training separates SEALs from all other U.S. military special ops teams.

The SEAL candidates will learn to SCUBA dive while under fire. They must be very comfortable in the water to handle this challenge.

The SEAL candidates also learn how to use diving as transportation. This skill allows SEALs to go from a ship to a mission location all underwater.

Third Phase

TRAINING FOCUS: land warfare
TRAINING LENGTH: seven weeks
TRAINING LOCATION: Coronado, California

Physical training continues in the third phase of BUD/S. The third phase focuses on skills needed in land-based combat. The men also still run, swim, and do obstacle courses. Each time, their completion times must improve or they will be dropped from SEAL training. In the third phase, candidates learn:

to navigate unfamiliar territory.

to patrol for enemies or dangerous weapons.

to enter combat by rappelling from rooftops or fast-roping from helicopters.

better shooting techniques.

to handle explosives.

BY THE END OF PHASE THREE, THE MEN ARE TOUGH, CONFIDENT, SKILLED MILITARY MEN. BUT THEY ARE NOT NAVY SEALs YET.

navigate—to steer a course

JUMP SCHOOL

Navy SEALs must be able to enter a combat zone by any way necessary. Jump school teaches SEAL trainees how to enter from the air.

One parachuting technique SEAL candidates learn is called High Altitude/High Opening (HAHO) jumping. In this type of jump, sailors jump from at least 30,000 feet (9,144 m). Shortly after jumping, they open their parachutes. They make a zigzag pattern as they descend to stay on target. This type of jump allows SEALs to cross enemy lines without putting the airplane in danger of being spotted.

High-altitude jumping is very dangerous. The men must wear oxygen masks to protect themselves from passing out. They also wear cold-weather gear to keep them safe in the cold temperatures.

Another technique is called High Altitude/Low Opening (HALO). In this type of jump, the men jump very close to the target from at least 36,000 feet (11,000 m). They free fall straight down for as long as possible to avoid detection by enemies.

HIGH ALTITUDE/ HIGH OPENING

HIGH ALTITUDE/ LOW OPENING

36,000 ft

Each jumper wears a device called an FF2. This device will automatically open the jumper's parachute if it hasn't opened before a preset altitude.

Fact

The Navy SEALs' training slogan is, "The only easy day was yesterday."

25

SQT SEAL QUALIFICATION TRAINING

The final step to becoming a SEAL is to pass SEAL Qualification Training (SQT). In this 26-week course, SEAL candidates learn how to work as a team on missions. They fire every weapon in the official SEAL arsenal.

SURVIVAL, EVASION, RESISTANCE, AND ESCAPE (SERE)

SQT trainees learn what to do in case they are caught by the enemy. They spend five days in a classroom learning survival skills. Then they spend five days doing a field exercise in which each man is "captured." The men learn what it might be like if they were ever captured as prisoners of war.

COMBAT SWIMMER

Combat swimmer training is a three-week course in SQT. In this training sailors become experts at SEAL missions in the water. They learn to do underwater reconnaissance missions. They also become experts at attaching mines to enemy ships and sneaking into harbors undetected.

COLD WEATHER/ MOUNTAINEERING

For 28 days, sailors train in Kodiak, Alaska. Students learn to survive in a cold mountain environment. They build shelters and start fires using what they find around them. They also learn how to navigate the rough land with compasses and **GPS**.

LIVE-FIRE TRAINING

Live-fire training takes place in the SEAL desert training facility in California. Sailors plan and conduct demolitions. They also practice with shoulder-fired rockets and small weapons. Another part of live-fire training is the Ruck Run. Wearing 65 pounds (29 kg) of gear, SEAL candidates must run 13 miles (21 km). The men must pass this test or they will not pass SQT.

Seal Trident

Each year about 1,000 men begin SEAL training. But only about 250 make it all the way through the pipeline. Those who do are awarded the SEAL trident pin. Each part of the pin has meaning related to the SEALs.

- The anchor and the trident symbolize the sea.
- The eagle stands for air.
- The pistol symbolizes land.

AFTER SQT

Once a sailor is awarded his pin, he is a Navy SEAL. He is immediately assigned to one of eight SEAL teams to begin preparing for missions.

GPS—an electronic tool that uses satellites to find the location of an object; GPS stands for Global Positioning System

Chapter 4

WEAPONS

Every mission has different needs, so SEALs must be familiar with several weapons. Here are just a few of the weapons SEALs may carry with them.

M4A1 CARBINE ASSAULT RIFLE

Weight: 5.56 pounds (2.5 kg)

The M4A1 is the primary weapon of SEALs. It fires 700 to 900 rounds per minute. It can easily be converted into a shotgun or grenade launcher. The M4A1 works well in close-quarters combat.

At the Top of the Scale

On top of their regular military pay, SEALs receive a $15,000 bonus when they make it onto the team. They also receive extra pay when missions require them to dive, parachute, or work with explosives. SEALs are the highest paid of all the U.S. special ops teams.

HK MP5 SUBMACHINE GUN

Weight: 6.47 pounds (2.9 kg)

SEALs use the MP5 for counterterrorism, hostage rescues, and close-quarters combat. It can be used to fire a single shot, three-round bursts, or 800 rounds per minute.

MK15 SNIPER RIFLE

Weight: 27 pounds (12.2 kg)

The MK15 is one of the most accurate and dependable semi-automatic rifle systems ever made. It has a range of about 0.5 mile (0.8 km). It can be used to hit a wide range of targets, including tanks.

M240B MACHINE GUN

Weight: 27.6 pounds (12.5 kg)

In certain situations, SEALs may use the M240B. The M240 is effective up to 1.1 miles (1.8 km) and fires 650 to 950 rounds per minute. It can be mounted on many of the boats used by SEALs.

Fact

SEALs and other special ops teams may use the MK23 Mod 0 SOCOM offensive handgun. This reliable gun can spend two hours under 66 feet (20 m) of water and still fire with near-perfect accuracy.

hostage—a person held against his or her will

MISSION REPORT

SEAL OBJECTIVE: rescue the captain of a cargo ship being held hostage by Somali pirates in the Gulf of Aden

DATE OF MISSION:
April 12, 2009

SOMALIA

Africa

Rescue Site

BACKGROUND: Piracy had been a growing problem off the coast of Somalia. These modern-day pirates would take control of ships and demand **ransom** for their return. The Somali government was struggling to control the country, so it did nothing to stop the pirates. Other countries had sent naval forces to stop them with little success.

ransom—money or objects that are demanded before someone or something being held captive can be set free

Timeline of Events:

Wednesday, April 8—Four Somali pirates attack the cargo ship *Maersk Alabama*. Ship captain Richard Phillips offers himself as a hostage to save his crew. The pirates agree and move into a lifeboat with Phillips.

Thursday, April 9—Crew members on the U.S. Army destroyer USS *Bainbridge* speak with the pirates. The pirates threaten to kill Phillips if they are attacked.

Friday, April 10—Phillips jumps into the sea and tries to swim toward nearby warships. But the pirates quickly recapture him.

Saturday, April 11—A team of Navy SEALs is flown in. The SEALs parachute into the sea with inflatable boats. They are picked up by the *Bainbridge*.

Sunday, April 12—Looking through night-vision scopes, SEALs see a pirate hold a gun to Phillips. Three SEAL snipers each fire one shot, killing all three pirates at once. The SEALs quickly slide down ropes from the *Bainbridge* to rescue Phillips.

USS *Bainbridge* tows the lifeboat from *Maersk Alabama* after the rescue of Captain Phillips.

LARGE WEAPONS

Sometimes SEALs need larger weapons than rifles and machine guns. In these cases, they may use weapons that aren't officially part of their arsenal.

The M224 60 mm Lightweight Company Mortar System (LWCMS) is like a small cannon. Rounds are loaded into the **muzzle** and fired at targets up to 2.17 miles (3.5 km) away.

LWCMS STATS

Length: 40 inches (102 cm)

Weight: 46.5 pounds (21 kg)

Maximum rate of fire: 30 rounds per minute

The main section of the LWCMS is called the cannon assembly.

The mount on the LWCMS elevates the weapon to fire at high angles. It has two parts. The two front legs are called a bipod. The circle in the back is the base plate.

The LWCMS has two sights. A long-range site is attached to the front of the bipod. A short-range sight is attached to the cannon tube. This sight is used for firing the weapon when moving.

M136 AT4
ANTI-TANK ROCKET

The M136 has been used in many combat situations against armored vehicles. The weapon fires rockets that can push through 14 inches (36 cm) of armor.

How an M136 Rocket Works

When the warhead hits a target, the nose crumples. A sensor then activates a fuse.	The fuse activates a detonator, which starts the main charge.	The main charge fires and pushes the warhead through the armor.	Metal pieces and light effects inside the warhead spray into the target. The light effects produce a blinding light. The metal pieces destroy the inside of the target.

M203 GRENADE LAUNCHER

The M203 is a lightweight single-shot weapon that fires grenades. This weapon is not used by itself. It is attached to an M16A2 rifle. The M203 can hit a target up to about 1,300 feet (400 m) away.

Fact

Each LWCMS costs more than $10,600.

muzzle—the discharging end of a weapon
warhead—the part of a missile that carries explosives

TRANSPORTATION AND GEAR

Many SEAL missions take place on, in, or around water. SEALs use watercraft that are specially designed to bring them into mission zones.

Watercraft

MARK V SPECIAL OPERATIONS CRAFT (MK V SOC)

MK Vs have been used by SEALS since the late 1990s. The boats can carry five crew members and up to 16 passengers. With a top speed of 58 miles (93 km) per hour, these boats can get SEALs in

SEAL DELIVERY VEHICLE (SDV)

This vehicle is used specifically by the SEALs. It launches from a submarine underwater. This launch method allows SEALs to enter enemy territory without being seen. Each SDV can hold six sailors. Without a heavy load, it can go 21 miles (34 km) per hour.

SDV operators wear full SCUBA gear so they can breathe.

In 1990 SEAL teams were deployed to Kuwait to help defend the country against Iraq. SEALs used SDVs to find underwater explosives. In 16 days, SEALs cleared 27 square miles (70 square km) without Iraqi soldiers suspecting a thing.

RIGID-HULL INFLATABLE BOAT (RIB)

The RIB is a high-speed watercraft that can withstand extreme weather conditions. It is used to drop off and pick up SEALs from enemy beaches. The RIB can travel at a top speed of 52 miles (84 km) per hour. It can carry eight passengers or 3,200 pounds (1,451 kg) of equipment.

SPECIAL OPERATIONS CRAFT-RIVERINE (SOC-R)

The SOC-R is a high-speed boat that can carry four crew members, eight SEALs, and 700 pounds (318 kg) of gear. This craft's main use is to bring SEALs to and from missions in water areas. But it can also provide fire support to SEALs moving onto land.

Length: 33 feet (10 m)   **Top speed:** 46 miles (74 km) per hour

MOUNTS ON THE SOC-R SUPPORT M60, MK19, AND M2HB MACHINE GUNS.

The M60 machine gun can fire 550 rounds per minute.

The MK19 can fire more than 350 grenades per minute.

The M2HB machine gun is effective against low-flying planes and small boats.

In 2003 SEALs showed how useful RIBs and MK Vs can be. To keep Iraqis from destroying oil and gas platforms, SEALs were sent to take them over. Under the cover of night, four MK Vs and eight RIBs swooped toward two main offshore oil terminals in the Persian Gulf. As they reached the platforms, SEALs jumped off the boats and overwhelmed the Iraqi guards. The SEALs quickly took control of the oil terminals.

The Drivers

Navy SEALs ride on specially-designed watercraft to get to their missions. But they aren't the people who drive them. Special Warfare Combatant Crewmen (SWCC) take care of that. SWCC are specifically trained to navigate these crafts through enemy waterways. They are also trained to use firepower to support SEALs who leave the boats during combat.

SWCC go through a stressful, difficult training and selection process. But it is not the same training that SEALs get. Their training focuses on how to support SEALs in their missions.

High-Tech Gear

Navy SEALs use some of the most high-tech gear in the world. They use whatever they need—no matter the cost.

DIVER COMMUNICATION SYSTEM — UP TO $1,500

SEALs talk to each other underwater and with others on the surface with ease using the diver communication system. Divers wear a microphone attached inside their face masks. This microphone is connected to a cell phone system that allows divers to communicate with anyone within 6,562 feet (2,000 m).

REBREATHER — UP TO $15,000

With regular SCUBA gear, divers breathe oxygen from the tank on their backs. Then the air they blow out goes into the water, forming bubbles. Enemies could possibly see those bubbles. So when secrecy is a top concern, SEALs use rebreathers. A rebreather allows a SEAL to continuously breathe his own air supply so no bubbles are made. Canisters of different gases worn on the front of the body keep the air clean and safe.

TAC-100 DIVER NAVIGATION BOARD — $200

Navigating underwater is tricky business. SEALs use a navigation board to keep them on course. This device includes an underwater compass and a depth gauge. The gauges are backlit with an LCD light so SEALs can read them underwater.

SEAL Dogs

A surprising, yet incredibly useful SEAL tool isn't a tool at all. It's an animal. SEAL teams use highly trained dogs to sniff out explosives or find hidden walls in enemy buildings. These dogs are even trained to parachute out of aircraft with their human masters.

SEAL dogs wear protective gear much like their handlers. The dogs are outfitted with vests that protect them from knife slashes and bullets. Their vests also have cameras with night vision that help their handlers perform searches at night. In 2011 the SEAL team that found and killed al-Qaida leader Osama bin Laden used a dog.

Clothing
and Protection

SEALs' gear changes based on what the men are sent to do. Worn from head-to-toe, the gear is designed to keep SEALs as safe as possible.

Tactical assault gear is used when SEALs fight an enemy at close range on land.

SEALs take some weapons underwater too, including the M4A1 rifle. They carry a pistol strapped to their legs.

Each SEAL wears a life vest. This vest can inflate to keep the head above water.

SEALs wear wet suits that keep them warm and protected in the water. Their hoods and gloves are lined with a strong material called titanium.

Helmets don't only protect the men from bullets. They carry a communication headset with a microphone too. The helmets have mounts for night-vision monoculars, which are basically binoculars for one eye.

The camouflage shirt and pants are called the Navy Working Uniform (NWU). Over this uniform, SEALs wear a protective vest. A body armor plate is inside the vest. The vest also has several pouches for carrying ammunition, knives, and other items.

Assault gloves keep SEALs from burning their hands as they fast-rope from helicopters.

Each SEAL wears a SPIE harness over his body armor. This harness has a clip and strap on the back. SEALs can use the clip and strap to connect the harness to ropes hanging from helicopters. Then the helicopter can lift them away.

MISSION REPORT

SEAL OBJECTIVE:
capture al-Qaida leader
Osama bin Laden

DATE OF MISSION:
May 1, 2011

BACKGROUND: The September 11, 2001,
al-Qaida terrorist attacks in New York City
and Washington, D.C., began a large-scale hunt
for Osama bin Laden. The terrorist leader was
believed to be hiding in Pakistan. The FBI
placed him on its "10 Most Wanted List."

bin Laden's compound

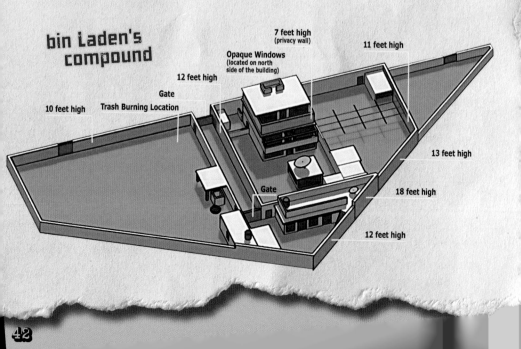

7 feet high
(privacy wall)

11 feet high

Opaque Windows
(located on north
side of the building)

12 feet high

Gate

Trash Burning Location

10 feet high

13 feet high

18 feet high

Gate

12 feet high

Timeline of Events:

September 2010—U.S. officials begin to suspect that bin Laden may be living in a compound in the city of Abbottabad, Pakistan.

mid-February 2011—Government leaders believe there is enough evidence to move forward with a plan to attack the compound.

early April 2011—SEALs begin practicing at a specially constructed compound.

April 29—President Barack Obama authorizes the planned mission to capture or kill bin Laden.

May 1—At night about 25 members of SEAL team six land in two helicopters outside the compound. One helicopter has trouble landing and clips one of the compound's walls. The SEALs then work in two groups to clear the main house and a guest house in the compound. They are met with small-arms fire. On an upper floor of the main building, SEALs find bin Laden and one of his wives in a room. After bin Laden makes a threatening move, the SEALs shoot and kill him. Four others in the compound are also killed in the raid. The SEALs then return to the helicopters. However, the damaged helicopter cannot lift off. The SEALs destroy this helicopter and all the SEALs leave on the remaining helicopter. The SEALs bury bin Laden's body at sea. Later that night, President Obama announces bin Laden's death to the public on TV.

Fact

The FBI has two "Most Wanted" lists. One is for fugitives and the other is for terrorists. Bin Laden was placed on both lists.

NEVER STOPPING

It takes a special kind of person to serve as a Navy SEAL. These men push their bodies and minds to the limit to prove they are fit for the team. Every day they put themselves in harm's way to protect their country. They are dedicated, loyal, strong, and smart.

THEY ARE **SEAL**s.

Always Training

SEALs are never done training. Enemies change and technology advances. SEALs have to be ready for anything. Here are just a few of the training programs SEALs may attend:

- ✓ foreign language study
- ✓ sniper assault
- ✓ tactical communications
- ✓ biological and chemical warfare
- ✓ deep-sea diving

"In times of war or uncertainty there is a special breed of warrior ready to answer our Nation's call. A common man with uncommon desire to succeed. Forged by adversity, he stands alongside America's finest special operations forces to serve his country, the American people, and protect their way of life. I am that man."

—*from the Navy SEAL Ethos*

GLOSSARY

assault (ah-SAWLT)—a violent attack

demolition (de-muh-LI-shuhn)—blowing up or taking down a structure on purpose

deploy (dee-PLOY)—to be put in place for a mission or battle

diversion (dye-VUR-zhuhn)—something that is a distraction

fast-rope (FAST-ROHP)—to quickly descend from a helicopter to the ground using a rope

GPS—an electronic tool that uses satellites to find the location of objects; GPS stands for Global Positioning System

hostage (HOSS-tij)—a person held against his or her will

intelligence (in-TEL-uh-jenss)—secret information about an enemy's plans or actions

muzzle (MUHZ-uhl)—the discharging end of a weapon

navigate (NAV-uh-gate)—to steer a course

ransom (RAN-suhm)—money or objects that are demanded before someone who is being held captive can be set free

reconnaissance (ree-KAH-nuh-suhnss)—a mission to gather information about an enemy

sabotage (SAB-uh-tahzh)—damage or destruction of property that is done on purpose

tactic (TAK-tik)—a plan for fighting a battle

terrorist (TER-ur-ist)—a person who uses threats, force, or violence to frighten or harm others

warhead (WOR-hed)—the part of a missile that carries explosives

READ MORE

Lunis, Natalie. *The Takedown of Osama bin Laden.* Special Ops. New York: Bearport Pub., 2012.

Montana, Jack. *Navy SEALs.* Special Forces: Protecting, Building, Teaching, and Fighting. Broomall, Pa.: Mason Crest Publishers, 2011.

Nelson, Drew. *Navy SEALs.* U.S. Special Forces. New York: Gareth Stevens Pub., 2012.

INTERNET SITES

FactHound offers a safe, fun way to find Internet sites related to this book. All of the sites on FactHound have been researched by our staff.

Here's all you do:

Visit www.facthound.com

Type in this code: 9781429687157

INDEX